Sideways Arithmetic
FROM
WAYSIDE
SCHOOL

X

**Watch out for more stories from
WAYSIDE SCHOOL**

and the MARVIN REDPOST series

other titles by the same author

www.louissachar.co.uk

LOUIS SACHAR

Sideways Arithmetic FROM WAYSIDE SCHOOL

Illustrated by Peter Allen

BLOOMSBURY
CHILDREN'S
BOOKS

BLOOMSBURY

First published in Great Britain in 2004 by Bloomsbury Publishing Plc
38 Soho Square, London, W1D 3HB

First published in the U.S. by Scholastic Inc.

Text copyright © Louis Sachar 1989
Illustrations copyright © Peter Allen 2004
The moral rights of the author and illustrator have been asserted

A CIP catalogue record of this book is available from the British Library

ISBN 0 7475 6912 6

Typeset by Tracey Cunnell

Printed in Great Britain by Clays Ltd, St Ives plc

10 9 8 7 6 5 4 3 2 1

All papers used by Bloomsbury Publishing are natural,
recyclable products made from wood grown in well-managed forests.
The manufacturing processes conform to the environmental
regulations of the country of origin.

TO DAN,
WHO TAUGHT ME TO PLAY CHESS
WHEN I WAS SIX YEARS OLD

CONTENTS

YARD TEACHER'S INTRODUCTION

AFTER WRITING 'SIDEWAYS STORIES FROM WAYSIDE SCHOOL', I RECEIVED OVER TEN THOUSAND LETTERS FROM KIDS, ALL WANTING TO GO TO SCHOOL HERE. THEY SEEMED TO THINK THAT ALL ANYBODY EVER HAD TO DO AT WAYSIDE WAS EAT ICE CREAM, DRAW PICTURES, AND WATCH MOVIES ABOUT TURTLES.

SO I HAVE NOW WRITTEN THIS BOOK TO SHOW THE TYPE OF WORK THAT IS EXPECTED FROM THE STUDENTS OF WAYSIDE SCHOOL. ONLY THOSE OF YOU WHO CAN SOLVE THE PUZZLES CONTAINED IN THIS BOOK SHOULD THINK ABOUT COMING TO SCHOOL HERE. ALL OF THE PUZZLES INVOLVE THE USE OF SIDEWAYS ARITHMETIC.

IT IS DIFFICULT TO EXPLAIN WHAT SIDEWAYS ARITHMETIC IS, EXACTLY. I DON'T UNDERSTAND IT TOO WELL, BUT I'M JUST THE YARD TEACHER. I CHASE THE BALLS THAT GO OVER THE FENCE. ALL I CAN SAY ABOUT IT IS THAT I ONCE BROUGHT A REGULAR ARITHMETIC BOOK TO SCHOOL AND READ IT TO THE KIDS ON A RAINY DAY. THEY COULDN'T STOP LAUGHING. THEY THOUGHT IT WAS A JOKE BOOK.

CHAPTER 1

SPELLING

Sue was very excited to be at Wayside School in Mrs. Jewls's class! She was surrounded by all the kids she had read about in her favorite book, *Sideways Stories from Wayside School*. She sat next to Rondi, who really was missing her two front teeth, just like it said in the book.

"Everyone take out your spelling books," said Mrs. Jewls. "It's time for arithmetic."

"Huh?" said Sue. She didn't know why you'd need spelling books to do arithmetic.

Mrs. Jewls wrote the first problem on the blackboard.

PROBLEM 1

$$
\begin{array}{r}
\text{elf} \\
+ \text{elf} \\
\hline
\end{array}
$$

"How much is elf plus elf?" asked Mrs. Jewls.

They all picked up their pencils and busily tried to figure out the answer. Allison raised her hand.

"Yes, Allison," said Mrs. Jewls.

"Fool!" Allison declared.

Mrs. Jewls smiled. "Very good," she said and she wrote the answer on the blackboard under the problem.

$$
\begin{array}{r}
\text{elf} \\
+ \text{elf} \\
\hline
\text{fool}
\end{array}
$$

"How foolish," said Sue.

Yet it wasn't foolish at all. Each letter in the above problem represents a different number between 0 and 9. The letters remain constant within the problem. For example, if **f** represented the number **8**, then every **f** in the problem would be replaced by the number **8**. But **f** isn't **8**. Can you figure out what number each letter represents?

e = ?   f = ?   l = ?   o = ?

An explanation of how to solve this type of problem follows.

Explanation

You don't start at the top. You don't start at the bottom. You have to look at the whole problem altogether. Then, like a detective, you search for clues.

The clue to the first problem is the letter **f** in *fool*.

$$
\begin{array}{r}
e\,l\,f \\
+\ e\,l\,f \\
\hline
\text{f}\,o\,o\,l
\end{array}
$$

Ignoring the first two columns for now, you see that:

$$
\begin{array}{r}
e \\
+\ e \\
\hline
f\,o
\end{array}
$$

Therefore **f** has to represent the number **1**. When adding two numbers, the only number you can ever carry is the number **1**. You now replace all the **f**'s in the problem with the number **1**.

$$
\begin{array}{r}
e\,l\,f \\
+\ e\,l\,f \\
\hline
f\,o\,o\,l
\end{array}
\qquad
\begin{array}{r}
e\,l\,1 \\
+\ e\,l\,1 \\
\hline
1\,o\,o\,l
\end{array}
$$

Since there are both letters and numbers, be careful that you don't confuse the number **1** with the letter **I**, or the number **0** with the letter **o**. Now, looking at the first column you see that:

$$\begin{array}{r} 1 \\ +\ 1 \\ \hline I \end{array}$$

Since you know that **1 + 1 = 2**, you can now replace all the letter **I**'s in the problem with the number **2**.

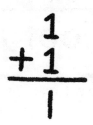

$$\begin{array}{r} e\,I\,1 \\ +\ e\,I\,1 \\ \hline 1\,o\,o\,I \end{array}$$

$$\begin{array}{r} e\,2\,1 \\ +\ e\,2\,1 \\ \hline 1\,o\,o\,2 \end{array}$$

In the second column you see that **2 + 2 = o**. You can now replace all the **o**'s in the problem with the number **4**.

$$\begin{array}{r} e21 \\ + e21 \\ \hline 1002 \end{array} \qquad \begin{array}{r} e21 \\ + e21 \\ \hline 1442 \end{array}$$

You now know that **e + e = 14**. Therefore **e** must represent the number **7**.

$$\begin{array}{r} elf \\ + elf \\ \hline fool \end{array} \qquad \begin{array}{r} 721 \\ + 721 \\ \hline 1442 \end{array}$$

The problem is now complete:

$$e = 7 \quad f = 1 \quad l = 2 \quad o = 4.$$

As you can see, when Mrs. Jewls asks, "How much is elf plus elf?" there is no way you can guess the exact answer she is looking for. You have to wait for someone in her class to give the "answer." Then you can figure out the numerical answer to the problem. So on the next question when Mrs. Jewls asks, "How much is egg plus egg?" you have to wait until the answer is given in class, and then try to solve the problem.

PROBLEM 2

Mrs. Jewls wrote another problem on the blackboard. "How much is egg plus egg?" she asked.

$$\begin{array}{r} e\,gg \\ +\ e\,gg \\ \hline \end{array}$$

"Scrambled or fried?" asked Ron.

"Scrambled," said Mrs. Jewls.

"Yech, I hate eggs," said John.

"Do you have pancakes?" asked Leslie.

Mrs. Jewls looked annoyed. "Don't talk with your mouth full," she scolded her.

At last Jason raised his hand. "Egg plus egg equals page," he announced.

$$\begin{array}{r} egg \\ + egg \\ \hline page \end{array}$$

Sue was very confused. "What page are we on?" she asked. She wasn't even hungry.

Again, each letter represents a different number. This time, what number does each letter represent?

a = ?   e = ?   g = ?   p = ?

An explanation of how to solve this problem follows.

Explanation

The clue to the second problem is the letter **g**.

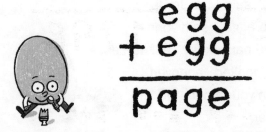

$$\begin{array}{r} egg \\ + egg \\ \hline page \end{array}$$

In the second column you see that **g + g = g**. At first you might think that **g** has to equal **0**. But in the first column you see that **g + g = e**. Since every letter has to represent a different number, both **e** and **g** can't represent **0**. If you try different numbers you will find that **g** has to represent **9**.

$$\begin{array}{r} e99 \\ + e99 \\ \hline pa9e \end{array}$$

Therefore **e** must represent **8**, and the rest of the problem is easily solved.

$$\begin{array}{r} egg \\ + egg \\ \hline page \end{array} \qquad \begin{array}{r} 899 \\ + 899 \\ \hline 1798 \end{array}$$

a = 7   e = 8   g = 9   p = 1

PROBLEM 3

"Listen carefully," said Mrs. Jewls.

"I'm all ears," said Sue.

"How much is ears plus ears?" asked Mrs. Jewls.

Todd figured out the answer to this one. "Swear!" he exclaimed.

$$\begin{array}{r} \text{ears} \\ + \text{ears} \\ \hline \text{swear} \end{array}$$

Todd's answer was correct but Mrs. Jewls sent him home because you are not allowed to swear in school.

What number did each letter represent?

a = ?   e = ?   r = ?   s = ?   w = ?

(**CLUE** Begin by trying to figure out what number the letter **s** represents. More hints can be found starting on page 81.)

Can you figure out what number each letter represents in the following problems?

PROBLEM 4

$$
\begin{array}{r}
\text{top} \\
+\ \text{tot} \\
\hline
\text{opt}
\end{array}
$$

o = ?   **p = ?**   **t = ?**

Be careful not to confuse the letter **o** with the number zero.

(**CLUE** Begin by trying to figure out what **p** must represent.)

PROBLEM 5

$$
\begin{array}{r}
\text{she} \\
+\ \text{eel} \\
\hline
\text{else}
\end{array}
$$

e = ?   **h = ?**   **l = ?**   **s = ?**

(**CLUE** First figure out what **e** and **l** must represent, then **s**.)

PROBLEM 6

mom
+ mop
yoyo

m = ?   o = ?   p = ?   y = ?

(**CLUE** After determining what **y** represents, determine what
two numbers the letter **o** might represent. Then see which
one works.)

PROBLEM 7

stays
+ say
trust

a = ?   r = ?   s = ?   t = ?   u = ?   y = ?

(**CLUE** Begin by figuring out what number the letter **t**
represents.)

PROBLEM 8

$$
\begin{array}{r}
\text{see} \\
-\ \text{as} \\
\hline
\text{as}
\end{array}
$$

a = ?   e = ?   s = ?

(**CLUE** If you have trouble dealing with subtraction, solve it as an addition problem.)

PROBLEM 9

$$
\begin{array}{r}
\text{yoyo} \\
-\ \text{pop} \\
\hline
\text{pop}
\end{array}
$$

o = ?   p = ?   y = ?

PROBLEM 10

$$\begin{array}{r} ewe \\ + \; dell \\ \hline woods \end{array}$$

d = ? e = ? l = ? o = ? s = ? w = ?

(**CLUE** First determine what numbers **w**, **o**, and **d** must represent. Then **e**.)

PROBLEM 11 – BONUS PROBLEM

$$\begin{array}{r} seed \\ + \; iced \\ \hline spice \end{array}$$

c = ? d = ? e = ? i = ? p = ? s = ?

(**CLUE** What two numbers could **i** possibly represent? Which one works? Is **e** even or odd?)

CHAPTER 2

NUMBERS

Sue was very upset. She had never heard of anybody adding words before. She thought it was the most ridiculous thing she'd ever seen. She would have thought it was funny if it hadn't upset her so much.

"How much is apples plus oranges?" asked Mrs. Jewls.

Sue couldn't take it any longer. "Fruit!" she screamed. "You can't add fruit!"

Everyone stared at her.

Sue sighed. She hadn't meant to shout so loud. "Everyone knows you can't add apples and oranges," she explained.

"Why is that?" asked Mrs. Jewls.

"You're not supposed to add and subtract words," said Sue.

Mrs. Jewls was taken aback. She had been adding and subtracting words all her life. "If you can't add and subtract words," she said, "what can you add and subtract?"

"Numbers," said Sue. "Like one plus one."

"What's one plus one?" asked Mrs. Jewls.

"Two," said Sue.

Mrs. Jewls was unsure, but she wrote it on the blackboard.

PROBLEM 12

$$\begin{array}{r} \text{one} \\ + \text{ one} \\ \hline \text{two} \end{array}$$

"No!" screamed Sue. "You're not supposed to write the words. You're supposed to write the numbers."

"What numbers?" asked Mrs. Jewls.

"One and two," said Sue.

"But there isn't a one or two anywhere in the problem," said Mrs. Jewls.

What number does each letter represent if none of them represents either a **1** or **2**?

e = ?   n = ?   o = ?   t = ?   w = ?

(**CLUE** Begin with the letter **o**. Is it even or odd? What's the largest number it can be?)

Everybody in the class was interested in Sue's unusual arithmetic. "What other problems do you know?" Mrs. Jewls asked her.

"There are millions," said Sue. "One plus two equals three. Four plus seven equals eleven—"

She was interrupted by the laughter from the rest of the class.

"Five plus two equals seven," she said.

The class was hysterical.

"Four plus eight equals twelve," she asserted.

Everyone was laughing so hard that Mrs. Jewls had to ring the cowbell on her desk. "Don't laugh," she said. "It's not nice to laugh at other people's mistakes."

"But I wasn't mistaken," Sue protested.

"I'm afraid that's impossible," said Mrs. Jewls.

If you try to solve the following problems as before, with each letter representing a different number, you will find that each is impossible.

PROBLEM 13

one
+ two
three

Why is this impossible?

PROBLEM 14

four
+ seven
eleven

Why is this impossible?

PROBLEM 15

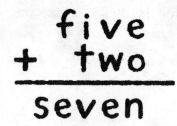

$$\begin{array}{r} \text{five} \\ + \text{ two} \\ \hline \text{seven} \end{array}$$

Why is this impossible?

PROBLEM 16

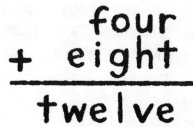

$$\begin{array}{r} \text{four} \\ + \text{ eight} \\ \hline \text{twelve} \end{array}$$

Why is this impossible?

29

PRONOUNS

While the other members of Mrs. Jewls's class worked on their paragraphs, Mrs. Jewls gave special help to Sue. She started at the very beginning, with the basic fundamentals of arithmetic: pronouns.

PROBLEM 17

"How much is he plus me?" she asked.

he
+ me
_____

CHAPTER 3

Sue was dumbfounded. "I don't know," she admitted.

"We," said Mrs. Jewls.

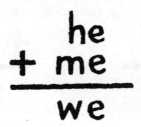

Sue studied the problem. In a way, she realized it did make sense. If she and her brother went to the store, she could say, "he and me went to the store," or "we went to the store." The grammar wasn't exactly right but at last something made sense. He plus me did equal we. "I think I understand," she said.

"That's wonderful," said Mrs. Jewls. "Then you can do the next problem. How much is me plus we?"

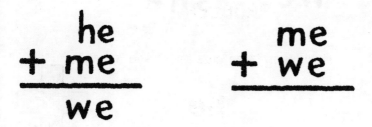

"But me is part of we," said Sue.

"No, me plus we is she," Mrs. Jewls corrected her.

$$\begin{array}{r} he \\ +\ me \\ \hline we \end{array} \qquad \begin{array}{r} me \\ +\ we \\ \hline she \end{array}$$

Sue stared blankly at the problem.

"Okay," said Mrs. Jewls. "So how much is he plus we?"

$$\begin{array}{r} he \\ +\ me \\ \hline we \end{array} \quad \begin{array}{r} me \\ +\ we \\ \hline she \end{array} \quad \begin{array}{r} he \\ +\ we \\ \hline \end{array}$$

Sue had no idea. She wondered what kind of stupid answer Mrs. Jewls would come up with.

"Sue," said Mrs. Jewls.

$$\begin{array}{r} he \\ + me \\ \hline we \end{array} \qquad \begin{array}{r} me \\ + we \\ \hline she \end{array} \qquad \begin{array}{r} he \\ + we \\ \hline sue \end{array}$$

"Hey, that's me!" Sue exclaimed.

Mrs. Jewls sighed. She wondered if Sue would ever learn. The three above problems must be solved together. For example, whatever number **h** represents in the first problem, it must represent that number in each of the other two problems. The same is true for the other letters. Each letter represents a different number. What number does each letter represent?

e = ? h = ? m = ? s = ? u = ? w = ?

(**CLUE** Although it is easy to determine what numbers **e** and **s** represent, it doesn't seem all that helpful. The key is figuring out what number **m** represents.)

PROBLEM 18

"All right, Sue," said Mrs. Jewls. "This is your last chance. If you can't answer this problem you'll have to go back to your old school."

"No, Mrs. Jewls," pleaded Sue. "Don't send me back there. You don't know what it's like." Even though she was totally lost, she still liked Wayside School better than her old school.

"I'm sorry, Sue, but in order to stay you have to answer the next question correctly."

"I'll try," said Sue. She concentrated extra hard.

"How much is moth plus took?" asked Mrs. Jewls.

Sue bit her lip. "Hmmmm," she muttered.

"That's right!" exclaimed Mrs. Jewls. "You did it! I'm so proud of you, Sue. Welcome to Wayside School." She gave Sue a Tootsie Roll Pop from the coffee can on her desk.

$$\begin{array}{r} \text{m o t h} \\ + \text{ t o o k} \\ \hline \text{h m m m m} \end{array}$$

h = ?   k = ?   m = ?   o = ?   t = ?

PARAGRAPHS

Solve the following multiplication problems. Be careful not to confuse the letter **o** with the number **0** or the letters **l** and **i** with the number **1**.

PROBLEM 19

```
      dog
    x  ad
    ------
      dog
     ado
    ------
    agog
```

$a = ?$ $d = ?$ $g = ?$ $o = ?$

An explanation of how to solve a multiplication problem follows.

Explanation

An important rule to remember is that one times any number equals that number:

$1 \times 4 = 4.$ $1 \times 1{,}000 = 1{,}000.$

And

$1 \times dog = dog.$

In this problem we see that **d x dog = dog.**

$$
\begin{array}{r}
dog \\
\times\ ad \\
\hline
dog \\
ado \\
\hline
agog
\end{array}
$$

Therefore **d = 1.**

Now look just at the addition part of the problem, replacing all **d**'s with the number **1**.

$$
\begin{array}{r}
dog \\
+\ ado \\
\hline
agog
\end{array}
\qquad
\begin{array}{r}
1og \\
+\ a1o \\
\hline
agog
\end{array}
$$

Two things become clear: **o = 0** and **g = 2**.

Now return to the whole problem and replace all the **d**'s with **1**, **g**'s with **2**, and **o**'s with **0**.

$$
\begin{array}{r}
dog \\
\times\ ad \\
\hline
dog \\
ado \\
\hline
agog
\end{array}
\qquad
\begin{array}{r}
102 \\
\times\ a1 \\
\hline
102 \\
a10 \\
\hline
a202
\end{array}
$$

We see that **a** times **2** equals a number that ends in zero. Since **a** can't equal zero, **a** has to equal **5**.

```
  dog          102
x ad         x  51
-----        -----
  dog          102
ado           510
-----        -----
agog          5202
```

The problem is now complete.

a = 5   d = 1   g = 2   o = 0

PROBLEM 20

```
  she
x  he
------
here
she
------
true
```

e = ?   h = ?   r = ?   s = ?   t = ?   u = ?

(**Clue** Notice that **e** times **e** equals a number that ends in **e**. What three numbers might **e** equal? Which one works?)

$$
\begin{array}{r}
\text{yak} \\
\times\ \text{so} \\
\hline
\text{sobs} \\
\text{yak} \\
\hline
\text{asks}
\end{array}
$$

a = ? b = ? k = ? o = ? s = ? y = ?

(**CLUE** Looking first at just the addition portion of the problem, what number does **b** represent? Looking at the multiplication portion, what number does **s** represent? What two numbers must **o** and **k** represent? Which one equals which?)

BOO! HOO!

$$
\begin{array}{r}
rye \\
\times\ be \\
\hline
are \\
eat \\
\hline
were
\end{array}
$$

a = ? b = ? e = ? r = ? w = ? y = ? t = ?

$$\begin{array}{r} \text{act} \\ \times\ \text{at} \\ \hline \text{less} \\ \text{yes} \\ \hline \text{clots} \end{array}$$

a = ?   c = ?   e = ?   l = ?
o = ?   s = ?   t = ?   y = ?

(**CLUE** The addition portion of the problem should give you what **c** and **y** each represent, although that doesn't give you any immediate help. Notice that **t** times **t** equals a number that has **s** as its last digit. Notice also that **s** plus **s** equals **t**. What are **s** and **t**?)

PROBLEM 24 —
SUPER BONUS PROBLEM

$$
\begin{array}{r}
\text{straw} \\
\times \quad \text{to} \\
\hline
\text{warts} \\
\text{straw} \quad \\
\hline
\text{chairs}
\end{array}
$$

**a = ?   c = ?   h = ?   i = ?   o = ?
r = ?   s = ?   t = ?   w = ?**

(**CLUE** This is the second hardest problem in the book. The following steps should help you:

1. Determine what number **t** must represent.

2. Determine **h** by looking only at the addition portion.

3. Determine **r** by looking only at the addition portion.

4. Determine **w** by looking only at the addition portion.

5. Solve the multiplication by trial and error.)

CHAPTER 5

RECESS

Ten kids gathered on the basketball court:

Maurecia	D. J.	Todd	Jason
	Joy	Sue	Deedee
	Dameon	Jenny	Myron

They had been looking forward to recess all morning so they could play basketball. Ten was the perfect number for playing basketball. They got ready to choose up teams.

Just then, Allison came by. "Anyone want to play freeze tag?" she asked.

"No," said Maurecia. "I'm going to play

basketball. We've got five for each team. That's the perfect number for basketball." Maurecia liked freeze tag, so if there weren't enough for five per team, she would have changed her mind and played freeze tag. But since there were ten kids ready to play basketball, she chose basketball.

"Me, too," said Joy. She always did whatever Maurecia did.

"I'm playing basketball," said Dameon. He would have played basketball even if there were only enough kids for four on each team. But if there were less than eight, then he would have changed his mind and played freeze tag.

"Who else is playing freeze tag?" asked D.J.

"Nobody — just me," said Allison.

"Well, in that case I'll play basketball," said D.J. "You need at least six kids to play freeze tag. If five other kids want to play freeze tag, then I'll play freeze tag, too."

"I like basketball, too," said Sue. She was new to the school so she wanted to be in the majority. So long as at least five other kids wanted to play basketball, she'd play basketball, too.

"Basketball," said Jenny. "You can't play freeze tag with less than eight people." If seven other kids played freeze tag, then Jenny would have played freeze tag, too.

"Basketball," said Todd. Todd loved basketball. He would have played even if there were only enough for two on each team. But if there were less than two per team, even Todd would have changed his mind and played freeze tag.

"Me, too," said Deedee. Deedee would have played basketball even if there were only two other kids who wanted to play. They could play "Horse" or "Around-the-World."

"Myron's my name, and basketball's my game," said Myron. He would have played basketball even if there was only one other person who wanted to play. In fact, "One-on-one" was his favorite game. The only way he'd play freeze tag would be if nobody else wanted to play basketball.

Jason was last. He liked basketball a lot, but he was secretly in love with Allison. "Okay, Allison," he said. "I'll play freeze tag with you."

This chart may help you with problems 25 through 28.

Maurecia — basketball, so long as there are five per team

Joy — whatever Maurecia wants to play

Dameon — basketball, so long as there are at least four per team

D.J. — basketball, unless five others want to play freeze tag

Sue — basketball, so long as five others play basketball

Jenny — basketball, unless seven others want to play freeze tag

Todd — basketball, so long as there are at least two per team

Deedee — basketball, so long as there are a total of three players

Myron — basketball, so long as he's not the only one

Jason — freeze tag, because he's in love with Allison

Allison — freeze tag, because she likes being chased by Jason

PROBLEM 25

How many people played freeze tag and how many played basketball?

PROBLEM 26

Everyone who wanted to play freeze tag followed Allison across the playground. Suddenly Jenny slapped herself on the forehead. "Oh, freeze tag!" she said. "I got mixed up. I was thinking of cheese tag. That's my favorite game. I hate freeze tag. There's no way I'll play freeze tag. I'll play basketball, even if I have to play by myself."

Now how many people wanted to play basketball, and how many wanted to play freeze tag?

PROBLEM 27

Dameon was Myron's best friend. "This is stupid," he said. "I want to play whatever game Myron plays." He went to join his friend.

Now how many played each game?

PROBLEM 28

"This is taking too long," said Todd. "We haven't even chosen teams yet and recess is almost over. I'm going to play freeze tag." He ran to the area where the other kids were playing.

"Newcomers are It," said Allison when Todd arrived. When the game finally started, who was It?

CHAPTER 6

SCIENCE, GEOGRAPHY, ETC.

Mrs. Jewls hated having to give her students grades. She thought that it was very boring to grade tests, so she usually did something else at the same time. She'd listen to records, cook dinner, take a shower, or often go bowling while she was grading tests. And many times, when she was in the middle of marking a test paper, something more interesting would come up and she'd leave the test and go do that. On such occasions, she usually forgot to finish up where she had left off.

This was fine until it came time to hand out report cards. Then she always had terrible problems. Her grade book was too soaked and soggy to read, and the tests were either lost or covered with food. It was almost impossible for her to figure out what grade to give to whom. Is it any wonder that she hated grading so much?

PROBLEM 29

Here are the answer sheets from a science test:

Paul's test
1. eggs
2. evaporation
3. Alligator
4. a potato
5. teeth

Todd's test
1. milk
2. transportation
3. Alligator
4. a kangeroo
5. teeth

Sharie's test
1. eggs
2. transportation
3. Crocodile
4. a kangeroo
5. ears

Jason's test
1. eggs
2. evaporation
3. Alligator
4. a kangeroo
5. teeth

Bebe's test
1. milk
2. transportation
3. Crocodile
4. a kangeroo
5. ears

Mrs. Jewls knew that somebody got all five correct but she didn't know who. She also knew someone got only four correct, someone got only three correct, somebody else got only two correct and one person only got one right. She lost the original test.

What were the correct answers?

PROBLEM 30

Here are the answer sheets from a geography test:

Nancy's test
1. Mississippi
2. New York
3. Tennessee
4. Utah
5. Arizona
6. Maryland

Joy's test
1. Mississippi
2. New York
3. Tennessee
4. Utah
5. New Mexico
6. Maryland

Calvin's test
1. Mississippi
2. New York
3. Tennessee
4. Ohio
5. Arizona
6. Wyoming

Ron's test
1. Minnesota
2. Alaska
3. Tennessee
4. Utah
5. New Mexico
6. Maryland

Eric Bacon's test
1. Alaska
2. Alaska
3. Alaska
4. Alaska
5. Alaska
6. Alaska

Mrs. Jewls knew that Nancy got five right, Joy got four right, Calvin got three right, Ron got two right, and Eric Bacon got at least one right. What were the correct answers?

By the way, these are the questions that were asked.

1. Where does my aunt Nora live?

2. Where did my brother go on his vacation?

3. Where does my cousin Arthur go every Labor Day?

4. Where would I like to be right now?

5. Where was my sister, Carol, born?

6. Where did I meet my husband?

cousin arthur →

← aunt nora

sister carol

PROBLEM 31

Here are the answer sheets from a test in word usage:

Deedee's test
1. can
2. like
3. Can
4. lay
5. well

Eric Oven's test
1. can
2. as
3. May
4. lie
5. good

Kathy's test
1. may
2. as
3. May
4. lie
5. well

Leslie's test
1. may
2. like
3. May
4. lie
5. good

Jenny's test
1. may
2. like
3. May
4. lay
5. well

Mrs. Jewls knew that each person missed two and only two, but she left the only copy of the test questions at the bowling alley, so she doesn't know who missed what. What were the correct answers?

PROBLEM 32

Here are the answer sheets from a true/false test:

Maurecia's test
1. false
2. true
3. true
4. true
5. false

Joe's test
1. false
2. true
3. true
4. false
5. true

Allison's test
1. true
2. false
3. true
4. true
5. false

Stephen's test
1. true
2. true
3. false
4. true
5. false

John's test
1. true
2. false
3. true
4. false
5. true

All Mrs. Jewls knew about this test was that she remembered that Joe got a better grade than Maurecia. She also remembered that Allison got a better grade than Stephen. She couldn't remember anything about John except she knew he didn't get them all right or all wrong. What were the correct answers?

PROBLEM 33

Here are the answer sheets from a test on manners:

Dameon's test

1. Say, "You're welcome."
2. Shake hands
3. Say, "Excuse me."
4. Wash your hands
5. Shake hands

D.J.'s test

1. Wash your hands
2. Shake hands
3. Say, "Excuse me."
4. Wash your hands
5. Shake hands

Terrence's test

1. Say, "You're welcome."
2. Shake hands
3. Say, "Please pass the peas."
4. Shake hands
5. Wash your hands

Rondi's test

1. Wash your hands
2. Say, "Please pass the peas."
3. Say, "Excuse me."
4. Shake hands
5. Wash your hands

Mrs. Jewls remembered that Dameon got a better grade than D.J., everyone did better than Terrence, and no question was missed by everyone.

She also remembered the questions she asked:

- What should you do when you meet someone new?

- What should you do after someone says, "Thank you" to you?

- What should you do when you want some more peas but the peas are on the other side of the table?

- What should you do after you burp?

- What should you do before each meal?

But unfortunately she couldn't remember in what order the questions were asked. In what order were they asked?

PROBLEM 34

Here are the answer sheets from a test on the animal kingdom:

Dana's test
1. Turtle
2. Monkey
3. Hippopotamus
4. Rhinoceros
5. Giraffe

Eric Fry's test
1. Turtle
2. Monkey
3. Rhinoceros
4. Hippopotamus
5. Giraffe

Rondi's test
1. Giraffe
2. Hippopotamus
3. Rhinoceros
4. Monkey
5. Turtle

Allison's test
1. Turtle
2. Hippopotamus
3. Rhinoceros
4. Monkey
5. Giraffe

Stephen's test
1. Giraffe
2. Rhinoceros
3. Monkey
4. Hippopotamus
5. Turtle

Somebody got all five correct. Somebody missed all five. Somebody got only three correct. Somebody got only two correct. Somebody got only one correct.

These are the questions Mrs. Jewls remembers asking:

- What animal likes to swing through trees and eat bananas?
- What animal has a very long neck?
- What animal has a horn or two?
- What animal is fat and gray like a rhinoceros, and its name almost even sounds like rhinoceros, and it is even harder to spell than rhinoceros, but it *isn't* a rhinoceros?
- What animal carries his home on his back?

In what order were the questions asked?

PROBLEM 35

Here are the answer sheets from a test on the Presidents of the United States:

Joy's test

1. Franklin Roosevelt
2. Jimmy Carter
3. Abe Lincoln
4. George Washington
5. John Kennedy

Todd's test

1. John Kennedy
2. Abe Lincoln
3. Jimmy Carter
4. George Washington
5. Franklin Roosevelt

Deedee's test

1. John Kennedy
2. George Washington
3. Franklin Roosevelt
4. Abe Lincoln
5. Jimmy Carter

Joe's test

1. George Washington
2. John Kennedy
3. Jimmy Carter
4. Franklin Roosevelt
5. Abraham Lincoln

Leslie's test

1. Jimmy Carter
2. George Washington
3. John Kennedy
4. Franklin Roosevelt
5. Abraham Lincoln

In this test, Mrs. Jewls remembered that each person got only one answer correct, and no two people answered the same question correctly. In what order were the following questions asked?

- What was the name of Martha Washington's husband?

- What was the name of Mary Todd Lincoln's husband?

- What was the name of Eleanor Roosevelt's husband?

- What was the name of Jackie Kennedy's husband?

- What was the name of Amy Carter's father?

PROBLEM 36

Here are the answer sheets from a test on holidays:

Jason's test

1. Lincoln's Birthday
2. Valentine's Day
3. The 4th of July
4. Thanksgiving
5. Columbus Day

Bebe's test

1. Lincoln's Birthday
2. The 4th of July
3. Thanksgiving
4. Columbus Day
5. Valentine's Day

Ron's test

1. The 4th of July
2. Valentine's Day
3. Lincoln's Birthday
4. Thanksgiving
5. Columbus Day

Calvin's test

1. Thanksgiving
2. The 4th of July
3. Lincoln's Birthday
4. Columbus Day
5. Valentine's Day

Todd's test

1. The 4th of July
2. Columbus Day
3. Thanksgiving
4. Valentine's Day
5. Lincoln's Birthday

These are the questions Mrs. Jewls asked:

- On what holiday do you give your sweetheart a valentine?
- What holiday do we celebrate on July 4th?
- On what holiday was Columbus born?
- On what holiday was Lincoln born?
- On what holiday do we give thanks?

Due to the difficulty of these questions, each question was answered correctly by only two people and missed by the other three. Calvin only got one right.

In what order were they asked?

CHAPTER 7

LUNCH

Miss Mush was the lunch teacher at Wayside School. She had long arms and long legs. She had big hands and big feet. She had long fingers and long toes, too. She even had long fingernails and long toenails. (Her toenails were so long that they punched holes in her shoes.)

That was why they made her the lunch teacher. When she stood on her tiptoes she could reach higher than any other person at Wayside School. She was a terrible cook, but she was the only one who could reach the top shelf of the cabinet above the refrigerator.

PROBLEM 37

"Miss Mush, Miss Mush," cried Rondi. "My shoe is stuck on top of the tetherball pole! Will you get it down, please?" (She had been playing kickball with her shoe untied.)

"I'll try, Rondi," said Miss Mush, who was very glad to have an excuse to leave the kitchen. It smelled funny.

Rondi's shoe was balanced on top of the tetherball pole. One only had to touch it to get it down.

The tetherball pole was nine and a half feet high.

Miss Mush was six feet, two inches tall. If she stood on her tiptoes she could raise herself four more inches. Her arms, to the end of her fingers, not counting her fingernails, were each two feet, nine inches long. Her fingernails were three and a half inches long. Could she reach Rondi's shoe without jumping?

PROBLEM 38

Mr. Pepperadder was Miss Mush's assistant. He wasn't as tall as she was, so she always played funny jokes on him. She'd ask him to get something for her, and when he told her he couldn't reach it, she'd laugh her head off.

Mr. Pepperadder always smiled and laughed, too,

because he was a good sport and because Miss Mush was his boss. They ate lunch together after everyone else finished eating. They ate whatever was left over. They usually had lots to eat.

"Mr. Pepperadder," said Miss Mush. "Will you please get me the peanut butter." She covered her mouth to keep from laughing because she knew that the peanut butter was kept in the cupboard above the broom closet.

The knob on that cabinet door was seven feet high.

Mr. Pepperadder's toes were one and a half inches long, approximately. His feet were nine inches long. His legs were three feet long. His arms were two and a half feet long from his shoulders to his wrists. His palms were four inches long. His longest finger was three inches. If he stood on his tiptoes, could he reach the knob in order to open the cabinet door?

PROBLEMS 39-42

Everybody always said that Miss Mush and Mr. Pepperadder were terrible cooks, but that wasn't really true. The problem was that it was difficult for them to cook for a lot of people. When they only cooked for one or two people, their food, in fact, was absolutely delicious. But unfortunately there were 4,500 people at Wayside School, and the more meals Miss Mush and Mr. Pepperadder had to cook, the worse each meal tasted.

If they cooked 100 meals, the food would be excellent.

If they cooked 500 meals, the food would be good.

If they cooked 1,000 meals, the food would taste okay, but it would smell funny.

If they cooked 1,500 meals, it would taste as bad as it smelled.

If they cooked 2,000 meals, it would be awful.

If they cooked 3,000 meals, it would be rotten.

If they cooked 3,500 meals, it would be disgusting.

And if they cooked 4,500 meals, half the people who ate would have to go home sick.

They had another problem. The worse the food tasted, the less people would eat.

If the food was excellent, everyone would want to eat.

If the food was good, only 3,000 people would want to eat it.

If the food tasted okay, but smelled funny, only 2,000 people would want to eat it.

If the food tasted as bad as it smelled, 1,500 people would want to eat it.

If the food was rotten, then only 500 people would still want to eat it.

And only 250 people would still want to eat it if it was disgusting.

And only 100 people would still want to eat it when it was so horrible that half the people who eat it would have to go home sick.

These two charts may help you solve the next four problems.

The first chart shows how the food would turn out, depending on how many meals were cooked.

100 meals — excellent

500 meals — good

1,000 meals — tastes okay, smells funny

1,500 meals — tastes as bad as it smells

2,000 meals — awful

3,000 meals — rotten

3,500 meals — disgusting

4,500 meals — half the people who eat would go home sick

The second chart shows how many people would want to eat at the different taste levels.

---

excellent — 4,500 would want to eat

good — 3,000 would want to eat

tastes okay, smells funny — 2,000 would want to eat

tastes as bad as it smells — 1,500 would want to eat

awful — 1,000 would want to eat

rotten — 500 would want to eat

disgusting — 250 would want to eat

half the people who eat would go home sick — 100 would want to eat

---

PROBLEM 39

If they cook 1,000 meals, how many meals would be eaten?

PROBLEM 40

If they cook 3,000 meals, how many meals would be eaten?

PROBLEM 41

How many meals should they cook so that the most number of people eat?

PROBLEM 42

If they cook 4,500 meals, how many people will go home sick?

CHAPTER 8

TRUE OR FALSE

Mrs. Jewls believed that the most important thing she could teach her students was the difference between true and false. She thought it was much more important than any of the other subjects because if students knew the difference between true and false, they could do well on any true/false test in any other subject. She always said, "If you learn nothing else in my class all year, I'll be satisfied as long as you learn the difference between true and false."

Here are some of Mrs. Jewls's true/false tests:

PROBLEM 43

After each statement, circle the letter **T** if you think the statement is true, or the letter **F** if you think the statement is false.

1. The answer to this statement
is the same as the answer
to statement number 2.   **T**   **F**

2. The answer to this statement
is different from the answer
to statement number 1.   **T**   **F**

In order to solve the above problem, it is necessary to look at both statements, together. In the next problem it will be necessary to look at all three statements together.

PROBLEM 44

After each statement, put a triangle around the letter **T** if you think the statement is true, or the letter **F** if you think the statement is false.

1. Statement number 3 is false.   **T**   **F**

2. Statement number 1 is true.   **T**   **F**

3. The answers to statements 1
and 2 are the same.   **T**   **F**

"I can't figure these out at all," complained Myron. "I was always taught never to tell a lie and to trust my teachers. But you've lied on half the statements you wrote."

"I don't even know which word rhymes with blue," said Stephen.

"That's because you're both so stupid," said Joy. "I got a hundred percent."

Mrs. Jewls could see that Myron and Stephen were very upset. She didn't want them to give up. So she made up three separate tests, one for Stephen, one for Myron, and one for Joy.

PROBLEM 45 — MYRON'S TEST

After each statement, underline the letter **T** if you think the statement is true, or the letter **F** if you think the statement is false.

1. Statement number 2 is true.   T   F
2. Statement number 1 is true.   T   F

PROBLEM 46 — STEPHEN'S TEST

After each statement, draw a box around the letter **T** if you think the statement is true, or the letter **F** if you think the statement is false.

1. Statement number 2 is false. T F
2. Statement number 1 is false. T F

Mrs. Jewls told Joy to stay after school and that she couldn't leave until she got a hundred percent on her test. "That should take about two seconds," said Joy.

PROBLEM 47 — JOY'S TEST

After each statement, draw a heptagon around the letter T if you think the statement is true, or a decagon around the letter F if you think the statement is false.

1. Statement number 2 is true. T F
2. Statement number 1 is false. T F

While Joy continues to work on that, try and solve the following:

PROBLEM 48

1. Statement number 4 is false. **T** **F**

2. Statement number 5 is false. **T** **F**

3. Statement number 1 is false. **T** **F**

4. Statement number 2 is false. **T** **F**

5. The answer to this statement
is the same as at least two
of the above answers. **T** **F**

PROBLEM 49

1. The answer to this statement
is different from the answer to
statement number 5. **T** **F**

2. The answer to this statement
is different from the answer to
statement number 3. **T** **F**

3. The answer to this statement
is the same as the answer to
statement number 4. **T** **F**

4. The answer to this statement
is different from the answer to
statement number 2. **T** **F**

5. The answer to this statement
is the same as the answer to
statement number 1 **T** **F**

PROBLEM 50

1. Statement number 5 is false.   T   F

2. Statement number 1 is false.   T   F

3. Statement number 4 is true.   T   F

4. There is only one false
statement in this problem.   T   F

5. The answers to statements 2
and 3 are the same.   T   F

PROBLEM 51

1. Statement number 3 is true.   T   F

2. Statement number 3 is false.   T   F

3. Statement number 5 is false.   T   F

4. Statement number 5 is true.   T   F

5. The answer to this statement
is the same as the answer to
statement number 3.   T   F

decagon

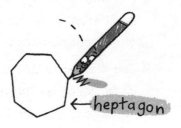

heptagon →

PROBLEM 52

1. The answers to statements 3
and 4 are the same.   T   F

2. At least four of the answers
contained in this problem
are false.   T   F

3. Statement number 5 is true.   T   F

4. The answers to statements 3
and 5 are different.   T   F

5. Statement number 3 is true.   T   F

6. The answer to this statement
is the same as the answer to
statement number 1.   T   F

(**CLUE**: Look at statement number 6. If it is true, what is the
answer to statement number 1? If it is false, what is the
answer to statement number 1? Now look at statements 3
and 5. Do they remind you of Myron's test? What are the
two possible answers? So what does that make statement
number 4?)

PROBLEM 53 — BONUS PROBLEM

1. The answer to this statement is different from the answer to statement number 5.　　**T**　　**F**

2. Statement number 10 is false.　　**T**　　**F**

3. This statement is true.　　**T**　　**F**

4. Statement number 7 is true.　　**T**　　**F**

5. At least two of the above statements are false.　　**T**　　**F**

6. The answer to this statement is different from the answer to statement number 9.　　**T**　　**F**

7. Statement number 6 is false.　　**T**　　**F**

8. Statement number 2 is true.　　**T**　　**F**

9. The answers to statements 3 and 4 are different.　　**T**　　**F**

10. The answer to statement number 3 is true.　　**T**　　**F**

PROBLEM 54 — BONUS PROBLEM

1. Statement number 10 is true.   T   F

2. The answer to this statement is different from the answer to statement number 9.   T   F

3. The answers to statements 1 and 2 are the same.   T   F

4. Statements 6 and 7 are both true.   T   F

5. Statement 8 is true.   T   F

6. Statement 5 is false.   T   F

7. The answer to this statement is the same as the answer to statement number 4.   T   F

8. Statement number 3 is false.   T   F

9. The answer to this statement is different from the answer to statement number 2.   T   F

10. Statement number 1 is true.   T   F

(**CLUE** Look at statements 2 and 9. Look at statement 7. Is 4 true or false?)

PROBLEM 55 —
SUPER BONUS PROBLEM

This is the hardest problem in the book. I bet your teacher can't figure it out.

1. The answers to statements 6 and 7 are the same.   **T**   **F**

2. Statement 1 is false.   **T**   **F**

3. The answers to statements 4 and 20 are different.   **T**   **F**

4. The answers to statements 3 and 20 are different.   **T**   **F**

5. The answer to this statement is different from the answer to statement number 19.   **T**   **F**

6. Statement number 2 is true.   **T**   **F**

7. Statement 15 is true.   **T**   **F**

8. The answers to statements 11 and 19 are the same.   **T**   **F**

9. Statement 10 is true.   **T**   **F**

10. Statement 13 is false.   **T**   **F**

11. Mrs. Jewls is allergic to strawberries.   **T**   **F**

12. Statement number 16 is true.   **T**   **F**

13. Statement number 12 is true.   **T**   **F**

14. The answer to this statement is the same as the answer to statement number 11.　　　T　F

15. At least half the statements contained in this problem are false.　　　T　F

16. At least half the statements contained in this problem are true.　　　T　F

17. The answers to statements 9 and 4 are the same.　　　T　F

18. Statement number 7 is true.　　　T　F

19. Mrs. Jewls's first name is Shirley.　　　T　F

20. The answers to statements 3 and 4 are different.　　　T　F

(**CLUE** Look at statement 5. What must be the answer to 19? Look at statement 14. What must be the answer to 11? Look at statement 8. Is it true or false? Look at statements 1, 2, and 6. What must be the answer to 7? What does that tell you about 15 and 16? Look at 1, 2, and 6 as a group. Look at 3, 4, and 20 as a group. There is more than one solution to each of those groups, but which one works with statements 15 and 16?)

CHAPTER 9

AFTER SCHOOL

Everybody went home except for Joy and Sue. Sue was still trying to figure out how to add apples and oranges, and Joy was working on the special true/false problem Mrs. Jewls had given her. She was talking to herself.

"If one is true, then two is true. But if two is true, then one is false. But if one is false, then two is false. But if two is false, then one is true. But if one is true then two is — Aaaaaaaaaa!" she suddenly screamed.

Sue looked up at her.

"Let's get out of here," said Joy.

Sue smiled. She hadn't made any friends yet at Wayside, and she was glad that Joy was talking to her. "Good idea," she said.

"We could go to my house and eat ice cream and draw pictures," Joy suggested.

"Okay," said Sue.

"And there's a movie about turtles on television at three-thirty," Joy added.

HINTS

All of the problems in this book can be figured out logically. However, if you're stuck, here are some more hints to help you.

Problem 3: s = 1.

Problem 4: p = 0.

Problem 5: s = 9.

Problem 6: o does not equal 0.

Problem 7: r = 0.

Problem 8: s = 1.

Problem 9: y = 1.

Problem 10: d = 9.

Problem 11: i = 9.

Problem 12: o is an even number.

Problem 17: m = 5.

Problem 18: m = 7.

Problem 20: h = 1; e = 5.

Problem 21: s = 1; o = 7.

Problem 22: e = 6.

Problem 23: s = 4.

Problem 24: w = 8; s = 2.

Problem 29: The best way to figure out this problem is to figure out who was the person who got all the answers correct. Remember that nobody missed all five. Also, notice that Paul and Bebe never gave the same answer. Therefore Paul could not have gotten them all right, because if he did, then Bebe would have gotten them all wrong. Similarly Bebe couldn't have gotten them all right, because then Paul would have missed them all. Check out what the results would be if Todd, Sharie, or Jason got them all right.

Problem 30: Nancy only missed one answer. The easiest way to figure out the problem is to figure out which answer Nancy missed.

Problem 31: Deedee missed question 3.

Problem 32: Compare Joe's answers to Maurecia's. They are all the same except for the last two. Since Joe got a better grade than Maurecia, what are the correct answers to problems 4 and 5? Now compare Allison's answers to Stephen's.

Problem 33: Compare Dameon's answers to D.J.'s. They are identical except for question 1. Since Dameon got a better grade than D.J., Dameon's answer for question 1 must be correct. Now compare Terrence's to Rondi's. Rondi got a better grade than Terrence, but Terrence got the first question right, and Rondi missed it.

Problem 34: Who got all five correct?

Problem 35: No two people answered the same question correctly. Therefore the answer to question 1 can't be John Kennedy. The answer to question 2 can't be George Washington. Three can't be Jimmy Carter. Four has to be Abe Lincoln. Five can't be Abe Lincoln.

Problem 36: Todd correctly answered question 1.

Problem 37: Miss Mush has a big head.

Problem 38: Mr. Pepperadder eats a lot.

Problem 48: 1 is false.

Problem 49: 3 is false.

Problem 50: 1 is false.

Problem 51: 5 is false.

Problem 52: 1 is true.

Problem 53: If 1 is true, what is the answer to statement number 5? If 1 is false, what is the answer to statement number 5?

Problem 54: If 7 is true, what is the answer to statement number 4? If 7 is false, what is the answer to statement number 4?

Problem 55: 1 is false.

ANSWERS

The answers begin on the following page. However, it is strongly recommended that you don't look at them. There is a tremendous feeling of satisfaction and pleasure in solving a problem yourself, but if you look up the answer in the back of the book, all you ever feel is, "So what. The answer is three. Big deal!" And once you look up an answer you can't ever un-look it up. You'll never be able to solve the problem yourself, for the rest of your life.

This is your last chance to change your mind! The answers begin on the next page.

If you do look up an answer, at least be careful not to accidentally look at any of the other answers. This is hard to do because you have to look at several other problem numbers until you find the problem number that you are looking for. And no matter how hard you try not to look at the other answers, or cover them up with your hand, they always seem to jump out at you. That's another good reason why you shouldn't look.

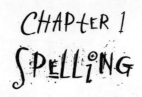

CHAPTER 1
SPELLING

Problem 1 Answer:

e = 7; f = 1; l = 2; o = 4.

Problem 2 Answer:

a = 7; e = 8; g = 9; p = 1.

Problem 3 Answer:

a = 4; e = 8; r = 2; s = 1; w = 6.

Problem 4 Answer:

o = 5; p = 0; t = 2.

Problem 5 Answer:

e = 1; h = 8; l = 0; s = 9.

Problem 6 Answer:

m = 7; o = 5; p = 8; y = 1.

Problem 7 Answer:

a = 7; r = 0; s = 8; t = 9; u = 5; y = 1.

Problem 8 Answer:

a = 6; e = 2; s = 1.

Problem 9 Answer:

o = 0; p = 5; y = 1.

Problem 10 Answer:

d = 9; e = 5; l = 7; o = 0; s = 2; w = 1.

Problem 11 Answer:

c = 2; d = 3; e = 6; i = 9; p = 0; s = 1.

CHAPTER 2
NUMBERS

Problem 12 Answer:

e = 7; n = 6; o = 4; t = 9; w = 3.

Problem 13 Answer:

A three-digit number plus a three-digit number cannot equal a five-digit number.

Problem 14 Answer:

The letters **f**, **o**, **u**, and **r** all must represent **0**. Since each letter must represent a different number, the problem is impossible.

Problem 15 Answer:

If you were going to try to solve this problem, the clue would be in columns four and five.

	5	4	3	2	1
		f	i	v	e
+			t	w	o
	s	e	v	e	n

The **s** in column five would have to represent the number **1**. The **f** in column four would represent the number **9**, and the **e** in column four would have to represent the number **zero**.

But if you look at column one, you'll see that **e** cannot represent **zero**. If it did then **e + o** would equal **o**. Instead **e + o = n**. Therefore, since **e** has to equal **zero**, while at the same time it can't equal **zero**, the problem is impossible.

Problem 16 Answer:

There are twelve letters in this problem. They all can't represent a different number.

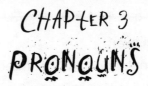

CHAPTER 3
PRONOUNS

Problem 17 Answer:

e = 0; h = 4; m = 5; s = 1; u = 3; w = 9.

Problem 18 Answer:

h = 1; k = 6; m = 7; o = 8; t = 9.

CHAPTER 4
PARAGRAPHS

Problem 19 Answer:

a = 5; d = 1; g = 2; o = 0.

Problem 20 Answer:

e = 5; h = 1; r = 7; s = 3; t = 4; u = 2.

Problem 21 Answer:

a = 4; b = 0; k = 3; o = 7; s = 1; y = 2.

Problem 22 Answer:

a = 8; b = 5; e = 6; r = 1; w = 7; y = 3; t = 0.

Problem 23 Answer:

a = 3; c = 1; e = 5; l = 2; o = 0; s = 4;
t = 8; y = 9.

Problem 24 Answer:

a = 7; c = 3; h = 0; i = 6; o = 4; r = 9;
s = 2; t = 1; w = 8.

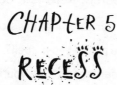

CHAPTER 5
RECESS

Problem 25 Answer:

Even though everyone except Allison and Jason said they wanted to play basketball, everyone played freeze tag and nobody played basketball. Isn't that funny? Myron didn't think so. Has something like that ever happened to you?

Problem 26 Answer:

Four played basketball: Jenny, Todd, Deedee, Myron. The other seven played freeze tag.

Problem 27 Answer:

Only four played freeze tag: Maurecia, Joy, Jason, and Allison. The other seven played basketball.

Problem 28 Answer:

Sue was the last person to change her mind so she was It.

CHAPTER 6
SCIENCE, GEOGRAPHY, ETC

Problem 29 Answer:

1. eggs; 2. evaporation; 3. Alligator;
4. a kangaroo; 5. teeth.

If you are interested, here is a copy of the test:

1. Which is better for throwing, eggs or milk?

2. What does e-v-a-p-o-r-a-t-i-o-n spell?

3. Complete this sentence: "See you later,—"

4. What can jump higher, a kangaroo or a potato?

5. What do you have more of, ears or teeth?

Problem 30 Answer:

1. Mississippi; 2. New York; 3. Alaska; 4. Utah;
5. Arizona; 6. Maryland.

Problem 31 Answer:

1. can; 2. like; 3. May; 4. lie; 5. well.

Here is a copy of the test:

Choose the proper word in each of the following
sentences.

1. My mother sent me to the store to buy a (may,
   can) of peas.

2. He is my friend because I (like, as) him.

3. My birthday is (May, Can) seventeenth.

4. You should never tell a (lay, lie).

5. They are in the backyard digging a (good, well).

Jenny didn't think that question I should count because she didn't like peas. Kathy didn't think question 2 was fair because she didn't have any friends and she didn't like anybody. Deedee didn't think question 3 was fair. "How am I supposed to know your birthday?" she asked Mrs. Jewls. So Mrs. Jewls decided to give credit for either answer on the first three questions. Then Leslie and Eric complained about that, so Mrs. Jewls gave credit for either answer on questions 4 and 5 as well.

Problem 32 Answer:

1. False; 2. False; 3. True; 4. False; 5. True.

Here is copy of the test that was given:

1. What word has more letters, true or false?
2. What was the answer to question 1, true or false?
3. Which word rhymes with blue, true or false?
4. Which word rhymes with zalse, true or false?
5. Which word begins with the letter t, true or false?

Allison argued that question 4 shouldn't count because *zalse* wasn't a word. Mrs. Jewls explained that it didn't have to be a word in order to rhyme with false. Allison agreed but pointed out that since it wasn't a word, she didn't know how it was pronounced. Even though it was spelled somewhat like false, it could have been pronounced like zoo. Mrs. Jewls had to admit she was right and gave her credit for question 4.

Problem 33 Answer:

The questions were asked in the following order:

1. What should you do after someone says, "Thank you" to you?

2. What should you do when you want some more peas but the peas are on the other side of the table?

3. What should you do after you burp?

4. What should you do before each meal?

5. What should you do when you meet someone new?

Terrence asked Mrs. Jewls not to count question 2 because he didn't like peas and would never ask for them. Mrs. Jewls took another point away from Terrence because he forgot to say, "Please."

Problem 34 Answer:

The questions were asked in the following order:

1. What animal has a very long neck?

2. What animal is fat and gray like a rhinoceros, and its name almost even sounds like rhinoceros, and it is even harder to spell than rhinoceros, but it isn't a rhinoceros?

3. What animal has a horn or two?

4. What animal likes to swing through trees and eat bananas?

5. What animal carries his home on his back?

Problem 35 Answer:

The questions were asked in the following order:

1. What was the name of Martha Washington's husband?

2. What was the name of Amy Carter's father?

3. What was the name of Jackie Kennedy's husband?

4. What was the name of Mary Todd Lincoln's husband?

5. What was the name of Eleanor Roosevelt's husband?

Problem 36 Answer:

The questions were asked in the following order:

1. What holiday do we celebrate on July 4th?

2. On what holiday do you give your sweetheart a valentine?

3. On what holiday was Lincoln born?

4. On what holiday do we give thanks?

5. On what holiday was Columbus born?

Bebe was very upset. She didn't think the test was fair. "How am I supposed to learn about holidays?" she asked. "Every time there's a holiday I have to stay home from school."

Mrs. Jewls realized that Bebe was right. And besides, holidays are supposed to be happy times. They shouldn't cause people to get upset. So she gave everyone an A on the test.

CHAPTER 7
LUNCH

Problem 37 Answer:

No, unless her head is smaller than a half an inch. Notice that the smaller her head, the higher she can reach. Is that true about everybody? Can people with small heads reach higher than people with big heads?

Problem 38 Answer:

Probably. Even though we don't know how much taller he would be if he stood on his tiptoes, it doesn't really matter. Presumably he has a chest and stomach, and they should easily give him enough height to reach the knob. Not only that, we know he must have a big stomach since he and Miss Mush usually eat a lot.

Problems 39–42:

This graph helps illustrate the answers to Problems 39–42.

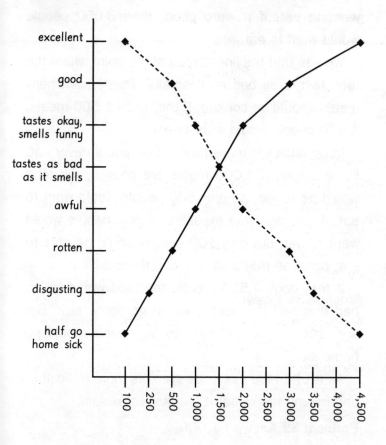

The broken line shows how the food would taste for how many meals are cooked. For example if 500 meals were cooked, the food would be good. If 2,000 meals were cooked it would be awful, etc.

The solid line shows how many people would want to eat the food at each level of taste. For example if the food were disgusting, only 250 people would want to eat. If it were good, then 3,000 people would want to eat, etc.

We see that the lines cross at the point where the food tastes as bad as it smells. That's how many meals should be cooked. If they cook 1,500 meals, 1,500 people would want to eat.

In no case will more than 1,500 people ever eat. For example, if 3,000 meals are cooked, the food would be rotten, so only 500 people would want to eat. If the food was excellent, 4,500 people would want to eat, but only 100 people would be able to eat, because that's all the food there is.

If they cook 4,500 meals, the food would be so bad that half the people would go home sick. But only 100 people will eat, so 50 people would go home sick.

As is often the case, the graph is more difficult to understand than what it is trying to explain.

Problem 39 Answer: 1,000.

Problem 40 Answer: 500.

Problem 41 Answer: 1,500.

Problem 42 Answer: 50.

CHAPTER 8
TRUE OR FALSE

Problem 43 Answer:

1. False; 2. True.

Problem 44 Answer:

1. False; 2. False; 3. True.

Problem 45 Answer:

They are either both true or both false.

Problem 46 Answer:

Either the first is true and the second is false or the first is false and the second is true.

Problem 47 Answer:

It's impossible.

Problem 48 Answer:

1. False; 2. False; 3. True; 4. True; 5. True.

Problem 49 Answer:

1. True; 2. False; 3. False; 4. True; 5. False.

Problem 50 Answer:

1. False; 2. True; 3. True; 4. True; 5. True.

Problem 51 Answer:

1. True; 2. False; 3. True; 4. False; 5. False.

Problem 52 Answer:

1. True; 2. True; 3. False; 4. False; 5. False; 6. False.

Problem 53 Answer:

1. True; 2. False; 3. True; 4. True; 5. False;
6. False; 7. True; 8. False; 9. False; 10. True.

Problem 54 Answer:

1. False; 2. False; 3. True; 4. True; 5. False;
6. True; 7. True; 8. False; 9. False; 10. False.

Problem 55 Answer:

1. False; 2. True; 3. True; 4. False; 5. True;
6. True; 7. False; 8. False; 9. False; 10. False;
11. True; 12. True; 13. True; 14. True;
15. False; 16. True; 17. True; 18. False;
19. False; 20. True.

NOTES